IS IT WRONG TO TRY TO PICK UP GIRLS IN A DUNGEON? ON THE SIDE
SWORD ORATORIA
TAKASHI YAGI
ORIGINAL STORY
FUJINO OMORI
CHARACTER DESIGN
KIYOTAKA HAIMURA
SUZUHITO YASUDA

CONTENTS

THE DAY BEFORE THE EXPEDITION
FINAL DAY OF TRAINING
NORTHWEST CITY WALL
quest 33. Expedition's Departure
GYAGA (CLANG)

GA (SLASH)
GA
GA
GA
GA
GA
GA

HE BLOCKED EVERY HIT...!
HE CAN PARRY...
GYA (CLANG)
BYU (FWISH)
THE DEFENSE WE'VE BEEN WORKING ON IS READY!

DO (CLASH)

...THAT WAS YOUR FIRST COUNTER-ATTACK.

...YES!

THAT'S IT...I GUESS.
PEKO (BOW)
THANK YOU FOR EVERY-THING!

I HAVEN'T LEARNED THE SECRET BEHIND HIS GROWTH...
...BUT...
...THAT'S FINE FOR NOW...
THANK YOU TOO.
THIS WAS... FUN.
...BECAUSE I REALLY ENJOYED THIS WEEK...

...WELL, KEEP UP THE GOOD WORK.
...I WILL!!
...GOOD-BYE...FOR NOW.

GA (CLANG)
GA
GA
GA
GA
GA
GA
GA
DUNGEON FLOOR FIVE
LOOSE YOUR ARROWS, FAIRY ARCHERS!
GA
GA
GA
GA
PIERCE, ARROW OF ACCURACY!

DOOOON (BLAM)
ARCS RAY!!
BO (BLAST)

IMPRESSIVE, LEFIYA.
YOU'RE REALLY GETTING THE HANG OF CONCURRENT CASTING...
HUH? EH HEH HEH...
ONLY THANKS TO RIVERIA-SAMA'S DAILY LESSONS...
...AND TRAINING SESSIONS FROM BOTH YOU AND FILVIS-SAN.
AIZ-SAN... I'M DOING MY BEST!
ALL SO I CAN SUPPORT YOU AND THE OTHERS ON THE EXPEDITION.
YEAH...

...AIZ-SAN...
...WHAT OF THAT HUMAN BOY?
HE'S ALSO BEEN TRYING VERY HARD.
...I SEE...
AIZ-SAN, PLEASE RETURN HOME WITHOUT ME.
I WOULD LIKE TO DO SOME FINE-TUNING ON MY OWN.
...SURE. DON'T PUSH YOURSELF TOO HARD, OKAY?

...WHEW...
PERHAPS I STAYED A BIT TOO LONG...

AH!
BATTARI (BUMP)

MU (IRK)

UHH...

I WON'T LOSE TO YOU!!
BISHI (JAB)
!?
TA (TMP) TA TA TA TA

LOKI FAMILIA'S
HOME
TWILIGHT MANOR

IF YOU WOULD, PLEASE, LOKIII!
ZORO (CHATTER)
ZORO

THANK YOU SO MUCH!
FER CRYIN' OUT LOUD! JUST HOW MANY OF YOU GUYS ARE OUT THERE!?

HOW COULD THIS MANY OF YA NEED STATUS UPDATES !!?
THE EXPE-DITION'S TOMOR-ROW!!
DON'T TRAIN UP TO THE LAST MINUTE! GOOD GRIEF!

GODS DAMMIT. DON'T EVEN HAVE TIME TO COP A FEW FEELS!!!

PEKO (BOW)
THANKS A BUNCH.
IS...
IS IT... OVER...?
HFF...
HFF...

YO, LOKI.
UPDATE MY STATUS, WILL YA?

GUH... BEEEEETE ...
GUTA (FLOP)
CAN'T YA SEE...
... I'M DYIN' OVER HERE ...?
JUST DO IT!!

PI (TAP)
AWW... IF ONLY I COULDA ENDED ON SOMEONE LIKE AIZ-TAN...
SCREW YOU! NOW GET ON WITH IT!

COMIN HERE AFTER EVERY-ONE ELS ALREAD LEFT...
YA KEEP-ING YOUR TRAINING A SECRET, ARE YAAA?
HYOI (POKE)
HYOI
HOW THE HELL'D YOU KNOW...?
GEH-HEE-HEE! THAT'S MY LITTLE SECRET.

I BET SOME OF THOSE KIDS WHO'RE SCARED OF YA WOULD FEEL MORE COM-FORTABLE AROUND YA...
...IF THEY LEARNED YOU ACTUALLY TRAIN HARD.
TOUGH ON THE OUTSIDE, SOFT ON THE INSIDE.
THAT'D HELP YA FIT IN, NO?

HAH!
WHAT DO I CARE ABOUT MAKING FRIENDS WITH WEAK-LINGS?

IT'S US STRONG FOLKS' DUTY TO LOOK DOWN ON THE SMALL FRIES.
OUR RIGHT.

IF WE DON'T LAUGH AND SPIT ON 'EM, WHO WILL?
OTHER-WISE, WE'LL JUST END UP WITH A BUNCHA IDIOTS WHO DON'T KNOW THEIR PLACE.

YER ABILITIES HAVE REALLY SHOT UP, BETE!
BY HOW MUCH ?
'BOUT THREE POINTS.
SHOT UP, MY ASS! THAT'S NOTHING!!
NAH, COME ON! FOR A LEVEL FIVE TO GET THESE KINDA RESULTS ON THEIR OWN, THAT'S REALLY SOMETHIN'!

...YEAH, YEAH, BETE. YOU'RE A TOUGH GUY...

I WANNA ASK THAT TOUGH GUY FOR A FAVOR ...
WITH THE EX-PEDITION STARTIN' TOMOR-ROW...
...PROTECT EVER'BODY, WOULD YA?

THEY MAY BE CHUMPS, BUT THEY AIN'T COWARDS.
THEY CAN TAKE CARE OF THEM-SELVES.
...HAAH.
PASA (PULL:)
YOU DIDN'T CHOOSE A BUNCHA TRASH...
...YOU OLD HAG.

—THE MORNING...
CHA (SHING)
...OF THE EXPEDITION.
SHAKIN (CLICK)

LEEET'S DO THIS!
ポイ
POI (TOSS)
ポイ
POI
ポイ
POI
DO YOU HAVE TO BE SO LOUD? JUST SHUT UP AND GET READY.
THIS EXPEDITION IS OUR CHANCE TO CATCH UP WITH AIZ!
LEFIYA, I'M HEADING OUT.
AH! ALL RIGHT! GO ON AHEAD!
ス
SU (INHALE)
ハ
HA (EXHALE)
OKAY!

...
OY...
WHERE'RE AIZ AND THE OTHERS?
GOOOOD MORNING!
I THINK THE TWINS ARE IN THE MESS HALL...
...BUT AIZ IS STILL IN HER ROOM.
YOU BETTER NOT HOLD US BACK, GOT IT!?

HUH?
SHE'S SKIPPING BREAK-FAST?
TCH!
THAT GOD DAMNED WOMAN ...
THE WERE-WOLF CAME OUT HERE EARLY JUST FOR THAT?
...THAT'S HIS STRANGE WAY OF BEING NICE.

grow bolder like an iron-clad brigade
leader to his outnumbered lot.
YOU UP, FINN?
ガチャ
GACHA (KERCHAK)
...OOPS. DIDN'T MEAN TO IN-TRUDE.
NO, T'S FINE. I JUST FINISHED.

PREPARATIONS ARE COMPLETE. ALL SUPPLIES ACCOUNTE FOR.
AH. THANKS, RIVERIA.
HOW IS EVERYONE DOING?
I DON'T FORESEE ANY ISSUES. ALL ARE IN TOP PHYSICAL CONDITION...
...AND MORALE IS HIGH.
AIZ AND THE REST OF THE YOUNG'UNS HAVE FINALLY GROWN UP.
...REMINDS ME OF THE THREE O' US WAY BACK WHEN.
THE DA HAS FINALL COME
WE'LL TAKE ON THE UNEXPLORED DEPTHS LEFT TO US BY ZEUS AND HERA.
...IF WE PROVE SUCCESSFUL, OUR NAMES WILL BE KNOWN ACROSS THE WORLD ONCE MORE.

YOU HAVEN'T HAD ENOUGH YET?
THERE ISN'T A PRUM AROUND WHO DOESN'T KNOW YOUR NAME.
AS FAR AS FAMOUS PRUMS IN ORARIO...
...I KNOW ONLY BRINGAR OF FREYA FAMILIA.
AS FOR OUTSIDE THE CITY, I HAVE VERY LITTLE KNOWL-EDGE.
PRUMS NEED A CHANCE TO SHINE...
...AN OPPORTU-NITY TO WAVE THEIR BANNERS OF COUR-AGE.
IT DOESN'T END HERE.
NO MATTER WHAT AWAITS, I SHALL PRESS FORWARD.
GOOD GRACIOUS... JUST ABOUT THE SAME AS THE DAY WE MET.
MORE AMBITION IN THOSE PINT-SIZED BONES OF YOURS THAN SOME MEN GOT IN THEIR WHOLE BODIES...
...AND NEVER GIVIN' A DAMN WHAT PEOPLE THINK OF IT EITHER!
AND HERE I THOUGHT I'D MEL-LOWED OUT.
HA! DON'T MAKE ME LAUGH!

...TO THINK THAT THE THREE OF US, DESPITE ALL OUR QUARRELS...
...WOULD SPEARHEAD A DUNGEON CRAWL TOGETHER.
WHAT A FUNNY WORLD.
GAH!?
YER GONNA TALK TO ME LIKE THAT!? YA HIGH-NOSED ELF!
TSUUUN (FWIP)
SPEAKING TO YOU IS POINTLESS.
THIS IS EXACTLY WHY I CANNOT WORK WITH DWARVES.
YEESH, TALK ABOUT THE POT CALLING THE KETTLE BLACK.
WOULD THE TWO OF YOU JUST CUT IT OUT?
HAAAH...
IT'S YOU LOOKIN' DOWN ON ME I JUST CAN'T STAND!!
MUKA (ROAR)
KNOW YOUR PLACE, PRUM!
... FOR SURE.
...YOU SAID IT.

LET'S DO THIS, YEAH? IT'LL BE A BREATH O' FRESH AIR.
THAT'S WHAT LOKI USED TO SAY.
SHE HAD TO FORCE US.
ALL YOU TWO DID WAS SCOWL.
...THOUGH I'M GUILTY OF THE SAME.

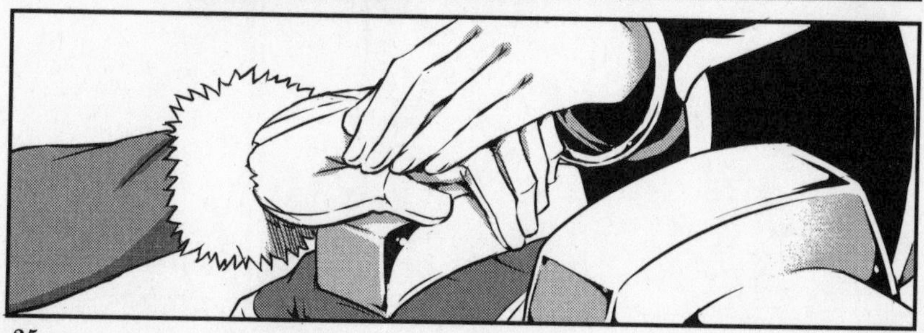

TO HEATED BAT- TLES.
TO AN UNKNOWN WORLD.

TO THE REVIVAL OF A RACE.

AIZ AND THE OTHERS WILL BE WAITING.
SHALL WE?
FINN ...
...HOW GOES THAT OTHER OBJECTIVE OF YOURS?
YES, YOUR SUCCESSOR ...
A BRIDE WHO CAN PRODUCE AN HEIR.
I'M NOT BLESSED WHEN IT COMES TO ROMANCE.
IF YOU TWO HAPPEN TO FIND SOMEONE NICE, DO INTRODUCE ME?

TIONE WOULD MURDER ME.
I POLITELY DECLINE.
SAME 'ERE.
HAT'S NFOR-NATE.

BASE OF BABEL TOWER, CENTRAL PARK
GAYA (CHATTER)
GAYA
GAYA
GAYA

OH-HO, SWORD PRIN-CESS!
BEEN A WHILE!
HOW YA BEEN?
TSUBAKI-SAN...I LOOK FORWARD TO WORKING WITH YOU.
JUST LEAVE THINGS TO ME! AND NO NEED TO BE SO FORMAL.
WE'RE ITCHIN' TO GET DOWN THERE TOO.

OH! THERE YOU ARE, BETE LOGA!
BETTER NOT BREAK THAT FROSVIRT OF YERS AGAIN! I DIDN'T SLEEP A WINK TRYIN' TO FIX IT!
OY! I GET IT! GET AWAY FROM ME!!

HOW FAIRS THE SWORD PRINCESS, HMM?
... LULUNE-SAN?
WHY ARE YOU HERE ...?

THOUGHT I'D WISH YOU WELL ON YOUR EXPEDI-TION... I GUESS.
YOU'VE SAVED MY LIFE MORE THAN A FEW TIMES ALREADY.

TAKE THESE. A LITTLE SOME-THING I LIKE TO BRING EX-PLORING.

JUST ONE PIECE WILL KEEP YOU FULL FOR A WHOLE DAY.

OH, DON'T WORRY. THERE'S NOTHING WEIRD IN 'EM.

キャラ
CHARA (CLINK)
FROM OUR FRIEND IN THE BLACK ROBES.
!

I HAD ASFI CHECK IT OUT, AND IT SEEMS PRETTY NORMAL.
...JUST SEEMS LIKE OUR FRIEND WANTED YOU TO HAVE IT FOR THE FIFTY-NINTH FLOOR.
TOSS IT IF YOU WANT. YOUR CALL.

BUT I'M NOT JUST HERE FOR THE DELIVERY, YOU KNOW...
...I REALLY DID WANT TO SEE YOU OFF.

ONCE YOU GET BACK, WE'LL GO FOR THAT DRINK, GOT IT?

WAS THAT LULUNE-SAN JUST NOW ...?
WHAT COULD SHE WANT WITH AIZ-SAN...?
LEFIYA-SAN.
A... AMID-SAN?
TAKE THESE... MY FAMILIA'S HIGH-MAGIC POTIONS.
THERE ARE ALSO SOME HIGH POTIONS AND ELIXIRS.
SHARE THEM WITH EVERY-ONE, WOULD YOU?
SO MANY...! THANK YOU SO VERY MUCH.
ALL OF ORARIO IS SUPPORTING YOUR EXPE-DITION.
MAY THE FORTUNES OF WAR SMILE UPON YOU.
...THANKS!
HEY, IT'S AMID!

—BROTHERS! SISTERS! THE EXPEDITION BEGINS NOW!
WE'LL BE SPLITTING INTO TWO PARTIES AS WE ENTER THE DUNGEON!
RENDEZVOUS ON THE EIGHTEENTH FLOOR AND WE WILL CONTINUE TOGETHER TO THE FIFTIETH FLOOR!
RIVERIA AND I SHALL LEAD THE FIRST PARTY...
...AND GARETH WILL LEAD THE SECOND!
OUR GOAL IS TO VENTURE INTO THE UNEXPLORED DEPTHS—
...THE FIFTY-NINTH FLOOR!

YOU ARE ADVENTURERS! WARRIORS NO LESS BRAVE THAN THE HEROES OF OLD!!
MAKE AN OATH TO THE LIGHT OF THE SURFACE...
CONQUER THE VAST UNKNOWN ...
...AND RETURN WITH FAME AND FOR-TUNE!!
SACRIFICES WILL LEAD TO NOTHING BUT FALSE HONOR!
...THAT YOU WILL COME BACK ALIVE!!

EXPE-
DITION
TEAM—
MOVE
OUT!!

ZAN
(THRUM)

THIS IS GONNA BE INTER- ESTIN' ...

COULD IT BE CALAMITY THAT AWAITS THEM? OR PERHAPS ...

—NOW...

...WILL YOU SHOW ME?

DUNGEON FLOOR SEVEN

AIZ! AIZ, DID YOU HEAR!?
HIGH SMITHS FROM HEPHAISTOS FAMILIA ARE COMING WITH US THIS TIME!
YES... I DID. IT'S WON-DERFUL.
HELL YEAH! SINCE THEY'RE FROM HEPHAISTOS FAMILIA...
...WE DON'T HAVE TO WORRY ABOUT THEM SLOWIN' US DOWN.

THERE IT IS—
BETE, WHY'RE YOU ALWAYS SAYING STUFF LIKE THAT?
DO YOU GET SOME KINDA THRILL LOOKING DOWN ON EVERYONE?
I HATE PEOPLE LIKE THAT!
HAH?
YOU THINK I ACTUALLY LIKE LOOKING DOWN ON BOTTOM-FEEDERS?
ALL I DO IS CALL IT LIKE I SEE IT.

I CAN'T STAND WEAK-LINGS. THAT'S ALL THERE IS TO IT.
SEEING THEM FLOUN-DER...
...MAKES ME SICK.
THAT SOUNDS LIKE NOTHING BUT THE ARROGANCE OF A STRONG MAN LOOKING DOWN HIS NOSE AT OTHERS.
TRUE! YOU WERE A WEAKLING ONCE TOO, YA KNOW!
I'M JUST SAYIN' THEY NEED TO KNOW THEIR PLACE.

...ONE'S PLACE...

THAT DAY AT THE BAR, HE SEEMED ABOUT TO CRY...
... BECAUSE OF WHAT BETE-SAN SAID, BECAUSE OF US.
HE LEARNED EXACTLY WHERE HE STOOD. AND HE HATED IT.

HE PULLED HIMSELF UP AFTER THAT.
IS IT THE SCORN FROM THAT DAY PUSHING HIM FORWARD?
IS THAT WHERE HIS FOCUS...
...AND HIS RECK-LESS-NESS COME FROM?

...IF THAT'S TRUE...
HA (GASP)

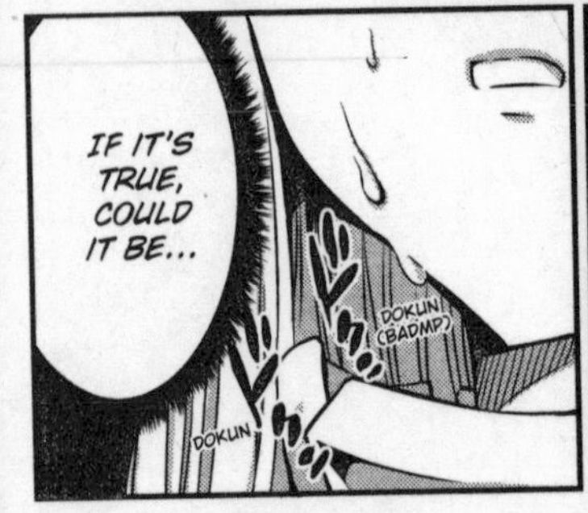
IF IT'S TRUE, COULD IT BE...
DOKUN (BADMP)
DOKUN

...THAT THE GOAL HE'S STRIVING FOR IS—
BETE-SAN!?
GAGAAAAN (SHOCK)
漢之背
STILL A BOTTOM-FEEDER, I SEE.
I'LL MAKE HIM NOTICE ME!
JACKET: LEADER OF THE PACK
WHAT'S WITH YOU, AIZ?
GURA (SWAY)
GURA
YOU'RE ACTIN' AS IF TIONA CLOBBERED YOU WITH HER ROCK-HARD HEAD.
SAY THAT AGAIN!?
PIKU (SNAP)
...FOUR OF THEM.
IN A HURRY TOO.

BATA (THUD)
BATA
HEEEEEY! WHAT'S WRONG!?
STOP THAT. PARTIES DON'T INTERFERE WITH ONE ANOTHER IN THE DUNGEON.
WH-WHO ARE ...!?
GAH!? TH-THE AMAZON !!?
TIONA HYRUTE !?
THAT MEANS... LOKI FAMILIA!! THE EXPEDITION!?

DOKE (SHOVE)
WHY'S IT ALWAYS ME...?
THE HELL ARE YOU DOIN'!?
GUI (PULL)
TH-THERE'S A MINOTAUR!!
... HUH?

I SAID, IT'S A MINOTAUR!!

THAT GREAT BULL OF A MONSTER WAS PROWLING THE UPPER LEVELS!
WE SAW IT ATTACKING SOME WHITE-HAIRED KID...
...AND WE RAN FOR OUR LIVES...!!

WHERE WAS THAT MINOTAUR!?
WHAT FLOOR DID YOU SEE AN ADVEN-TURER BEING ATTACKED ON!?
F-FLOOR NINE...

AIZ!?
WHAT THE HELL ARE YOU DOING !!?
DA (DASH)
IF THAT BOY IS THE ONE...
...FACING A MINOTAUR...

...HE DOESN'T STAND A CHANCE.

HE'S GONNA DIE!!

I'M SURE IT ALL STARTED...

...IN THAT MOMENT.

THOSE GOLDEN EYES...

...WERE LIKE A LIGHTNING STRIKE...

...THAT LIT UP THE DIM DUNGEON.

AND I FELL IN LOVE.
quest 34. The Adventurer Bell Cranell

HER NAME WAS AIZ WALLEN-STEIN.
PART OF ORARIO'S LARGEST GROUP, LOKI FAMILIA...
...SHE'S CALLED "KENKI," THE SWORD PRINCESS, AND IS ONE OF THE STRONGEST ADVENTURERS IN THE CITY.
COMPARED TO HER...
...I WAS JUST SOME COUNTRY KID WITH A DREAM TO BE AN ADVENTURER...
...WHO GOT TURNED AWAY FROM EVERY FAMILIA, NO MATTER WHERE I WENT.
HESTIA-SAMA FOUND ME WHEN I WAS DOWN ON MYSELF, AND SHE TOOK ME IN.
THE TWO OF US BECAME HESTIA FAMILIA...
...JUST THE GODDESS AND ME—THE NEWBIE ADVENTURER.

SOMEONE LIKE HER WAS WAY OUT OF MY LEAGUE...
...BUT THAT NEVER OCCURRED TO ME BACK THEN.
AS LONG AS WE WERE BOTH ADVENTURERS IN THE SAME CITY, FIGHTING IN THE SAME DUNGEON...
...THEN, SOME-DAY...
HAVING THAT DREAM MADE ME SO HAPPY...
...MY HEART WENT WILD WITH THE MERE THOUGHT OF IT.
THAT IS, UNTIL I OVER-HEARD THAT CONVER-SATION.

HE'S A WORM. A WEAKLING LIKE THAT ISN'T GONNA LAND AIZ WALLENSTEIN.
SUDDENLY, I WAS FACING A REALITY...
...I COULD NOT TAKE...
...HOW NAIVE—HOW STUPID I'D BEEN ALL ALONG.

SO FRUS-TRAT-ING ...!
MORTIFY-ING... !!

UNABLE TO EVEN SAY ANYTHING TO DEFEND MYSELF...
...BEING SO WEAK— I CAN'T TAKE IT!

THINK-ING "SOME-DAY"...
... HAVING A "DREAM"...
...OR BELIEVING "SOMETHING" WOULD HAPPEN IF I JUST WAITED.
I CAN'T FORGIVE MYSELF!!

I WON'T BE ALLOWED TO EVEN STAND BEFORE HER UNLESS I DO EVERYTHING I CAN!!

THAT'S WHEN I STARTED FIGHTING.
I STARTED GOING INTO THE DUNGEON EACH DAY...
...TRAINING AS HARD AS I COULD...
...AND TRYING TO CRAM EVEN A LITTLE BIT MORE KNOWL-EDGE INTO MY HEAD.
SO MANY PEOPLE HAVE HELPED ME ON MY JOURNEY.
THEY'VE SUPPORT-ED ME IN SO MANY WAYS.

IT WAS SLOW, BUT THINGS WERE CHANGING.
I WAS GETTING CLOSER.
AT LEAST, THAT THOUGHT...

OUR WORLDS WERE TOO FAR APART...
TRYING TO BRIDGE A GAP LIKE THAT IS HOPE-LESS.
I COULDN'T EVEN FOLLOW HER MOVE-MENTS...
...AND MY MAGIC MADE NO DIFFER-ENCE AT ALL.
LEVEL SIX... !?
IT SEEMS SHE DEFEATED A DEEP-LEVEL FLOOR BOSS ON HER OWN.
TO MY KNOWLEDGE, THAT HAS NEVER HAPPENED BEFORE.
YOU CAN'T LET THIS DISCOURAGE YOU.
WALLENSTEIN-SHI IS...SPECIAL.

THE DISTANCE IS SO GREAT...
I THOUGHT THE GAP WAS CLOSING, BUT SHE'S STILL SO FAR AWAY.
SO FAR...

I WAS ABOUT TO LOSE HOPE...
...THINKING THERE WAS NOTHING I COULD DO.
THINKING I'D SPEND MY WHOLE LIFE TRYING AND STILL NEVER CATCH UP.

SEEING HER FIGHT WITH MY OWN EYES MADE IT OBVIOUS.
WE WEREN'T TWO OF THE SAME AT ALL.
WHAT I'D BEEN DOING COULDN'T EVEN BE COUNTED AS BEING AN ADVENTURER.
GODDESS, PLEASE TELL ME.
MY DESIRE...
...MY HARD WORK...
EVERY-THING...
HAAH...
HAAH...
HAAH...

WAS IT ALL
FOR NOTHING...?

DUNGEON FLOOR NINE
ZA (SKID)

OOOOOOO (HOWLS)
BEAST ROARS AND BATTLE SOUNDS...! THEY'RE FAINT, BUT THEY'RE ON THIS FLOOR!
BUT WITH THE WAY THE SOUND IS ECHOING I CAN'T TELL...
... WHERE IT'S FROM !
OOO

!!
YORO (STUMBLE)

ADVEN-TURER... SAMA...
... PLEASE... HELP... !!

FU (DROP)
ZA

PLEASE SAVE... SAVE BELL-SAMA...!!
!
WHERE IS HE?
ON THE... STANDARD ROUTE... ROOM E-16...!

BA (CLATTER)

DO
SWORD PRINCESS, I CHAL-LENGE YOU..
DO
DO
DO
DO (THUD)
...WARLORD. THE CAPTAIN OF FREYA FAMILIA... ORARIO'S ONLY LEVEL SEVEN ADVENTURER ...!!
WHY...!?
ZUN (SHING)
WHY IS HE HERE !?
AN ENCOUNTER WITH A LONG-STANDING ENEMY ALONE IN THE DUNGEON...
WHAT BETTER REASON TO DUEL TO THE DEATH?
GU (GRIP)

!!
IS THAT IT?

CONSIDER THIS A WARNING.
GET IN OUR—IN HER WAY...
WE WILL KILL YOU.

WAS THEIR GOAL ALL ALONG...?
ARE THEY ACTUALLY TRYING TO—

COME, SWORD PRINCESS.

... GET ...
CHIKI (CLINK)
...OUT OF MY WAY!!
DO (LUNGE)
GYU (WHIRL)

HAAAAAHHH!!
GYU (WHIRL)
BA (CLANG)
BA
BA
BA
HIU (SWISH)

ZUKUA (FWOOM)
GO (WHAM)
—AH, YES. YOU RECENTLY REACHED A NEW LEVEL, DIDN'T YOU?
THOSE MOVES...
HE BLOCKED EVERYTHING!!?
JUST HOW STRONG WILL YOU BECOME, SWORD PRINCESS?

BOUUU
(SLASH)
—!!
A SWORD THAT LARGE FASTER THAN MY DESPERATE... AND STRONG!!
I WON'T BE ABLE TO KEEP UP!!
TEMPEST!!!

NGHHH!!
GYU (WHOOSH)
GAN (SLAM)
!!?
EVEN WITH AIRIEL !?

BAN
(WHAM)
DA
(TMP)
THE FAINT BATTLE SOUNDS FROM EARLIER ARE GONE...
IS THE BOY —?
GIRU
(WHIRL)
STAND ASIDE!!
GO
(ROAR)

GYA
(ZOOM)
LIL RAFAGA!!!

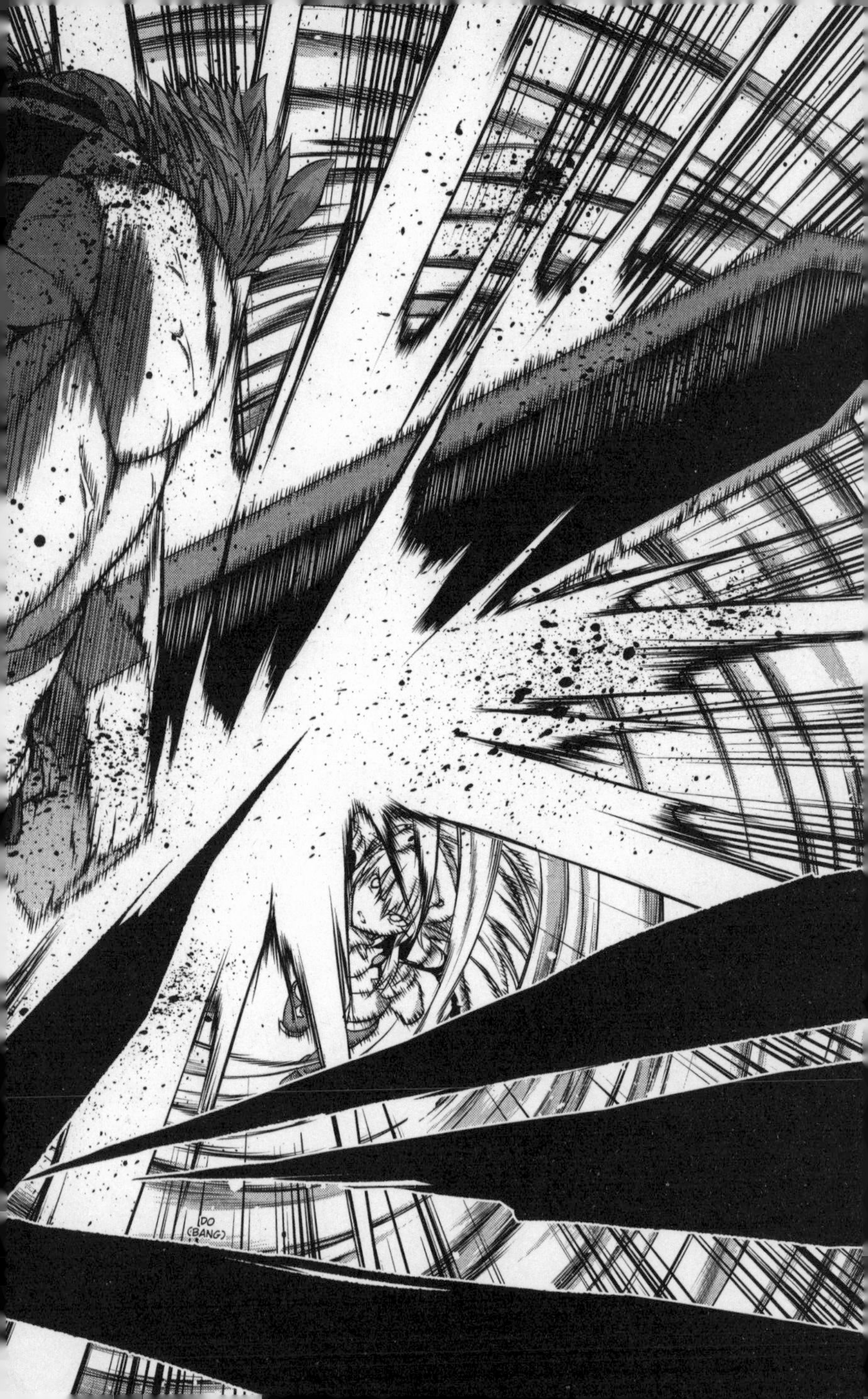
DO
(BANG)

HUURRRAAHHH!!!

BAO (BOOM)
ZA (SKID)
ZA
ZA
ZA
ZA
...HE...
...STOPPED IT...
HFF! HFF!
I HELD BACK JUST ENOUGH NOT TO BE LETHAL...
...BUT... EVEN SO...
OOOOOO (WHOOSH)
...I LOST...
...IN A CONTEST OF PURE STRENGTH.
THIS IS LEVEL SEVEN.
NO. THIS IS THE WARLORD.

THE MOST POWERFUL ADVENTURER IN ORARIO...
..."WARLORD" OTTAR.
FUOOA (HISS)
OUT OF MY WAY!!
DA ASH)

GAGA (CLANG)
GIN (SHING)

WHAT'S GOING ON HERE —!?
WHATEVER IT IS, WE'RE STEPPING IN!!
AMAZON, JORMUN-GAND...!

GA
GA
GA
GA
GA
NOW!!
BA (BURST)
NNGH!
VANAR-GAND!!
JUST TRY AN' LOOK AWAY FROM ME, PORKY!!
GAKI (CLASH)

GISAN (CLANG)
I'M THROUGH!!

ZA (THUMP)

AND HERE I WAS THINKING MY THUMB WAS AWFULLY ITCHY...
I SUPPOSE THIS IS ALL...
...PART OF THE BARGAIN?

HEY, OTTAR.
...FINN?

RIVERIA! HELP THAT PRUM-CHAN, OKAY!?
WE STILL HAVE NO IDEA WHAT THE HELL'S GOING ON!
たったー
TATTA (HOP)
WAIT ...

AH... WHY IS IT ALWAYS THOSE TWO?

IS IT SAFE TO ASSUME THIS...
...IS NOT ONLY THE WILL OF YOUR FAMILIA BUT YOUR GODDESS AS WELL?
IS LADY FREYA HOPING FOR AN ALL-OUT WAR?

...I ACTED INDE-PENDENT-LY.

SO LONG AS YOU HAVE YOUR LITTLE CLIQUE ...
...I HAVE NO CHANCE OF WIN-NING.
GOKON (THUD)
GOOD TO KNOW.
WE'RE NOT KEEN ON TAKING UP ARMS AGAINST YOU EITHER.

WASTING THIS OP-PORTUNITY TO FINISH ME OFF...
YOU WILL RE-GRET IT.

YOU ARE OBLIVIOUS TO YOUR OWN INCOMPE-TENCE.

REMOVE YOUR SHELL.
RENOUNCE ALL OTHERS...
...AND CONFRONT THE ADVENTURE.
FOCUS ON NOTHING BUT THE PATH AHEAD.
ONLY THEN CAN YOU WIN HER FAVOR.

ARE YOU ALL RIGHT?
YOU FOUGHT WELL.
YOU FOUGHT VERY WELL.

I'LL TAKE CARE OF THINGS NOW.

AIZ-SAN...
IT'S THE SAME.
EXACTLY THE SAME AS LAST TIME.

I'M STILL JUST A WEAKLING THAT...

...HAS TO BE...

...SAVED BY HER AGAIN.

GET UP.
GET UP!
STAND UP!!
MY IDOL...IS STANDING RIGHT THERE!!
IF I DON'T STAND UP RIGHT NOW...
I'VE HAD ENOUGH OF BEING PATHETIC!
I MADE UP MY MIND TO BE STRONG!!

...IF I DON'T REACH FOR NEW HEIGHTS RIGHT NOW...
...WHEN WILL I EVER GET THERE!?

DOKUN
DOKUN
HE SHOULDN'T BE ABLE TO STAND.
DOKUN
HE CAN'T DEFEAT THIS FOE.
THIS IS A FIGHT HE CAN'T WIN.

SO WHY WOULD HE...

...STILL PICK UP A SWORD—?

DOKUN
WE SHARE A BLACK FLAME.

YOU'LL CHANGE TOO.
YOUR CLEAR AND PURE EYES...
...WILL BECOME STAINED WITH HATRED AND FURY.
NO!
I CAN'T LET YOU!
—NOT... AGAIN ...!

DON'T BECOME LIKE ME!
I WON'T BE...
...SAVED AGAIN BY AIZ WALLEN-STEIN!!

...
HOW...?
HIS GAZE...
...IS COM-
PLETELY
CLEAR.
ALL THAT'S
THERE...
...IS
BLINDING,
STRAIGHT-
FORWARD
DETERMINA-
TION.
—!
WAI—
!

STAY THERE, AIZ.

I DON'T UNDERSTAND...
...WHAT'S MAKING YOU DO THIS.
BECAUSE OF YOU...
BECAUE THAT MOMENT KEEPS BURNING BRIGHT IN MY HEART...
...BUT I GUESS I DO UNDERSTAND.
LET'S GO ON AN ADVEN-TURE...
...TO SATISFY THIS UNRE-LENTING DESIRE.
YOU STILL HAVE YOUR PURITY...
...SO—

THIS WILL BE...
IS BORN.

—NOW BEFORE MY EYES...

...A TRUE ADVENTURER

Is it Wrong to Try to Pick Up Girls in a Dungeon? On the Side

Sword Oratoria

STAY THERE, AIZ.

I WON'T BE SAVED AGAIN
BY AIZ WALLENSTEIN!

I JUST STAND AND WATCH.

AS I WATCH THIS BOY TAKE HIS FIRST STEP ON THE PATH TO BECOMING A HERO...

...I CAN'T MOVE AN INCH.
quest 35. The Hero Argonaut

OUTTA THE WAY, AIZ!! I'VE GOT THIS!
YO! WHAT'RE YOU JUST STANDING AROUND...
...FOR...?

HUH...? ISN'T THAT ...?
...WHO SAID HE WAS LEVEL ONE?
IF MEMORY SERVES ME COR-RECTLY...
...ISN'T THAT THE SAME KID...
...BETE CALLED A COMPLETE BEGINNER JUST A MONTH AGO?

AHHHHHHH!!!
GWROOOOOO

IT WASN'T ALL FOR NOTHING!
EVERY-THING I'VE DONE...
...HASN'T BEEN IN VAIN!!
I WON'T LET ALL MY WORK GO TO WASTE!!!

HIT IT WITH EVERY-THING!
EVERY-THING I HAVE!

GIGI (SLASH)
THE STATUS THE GOD-DESS GAVE ME.
THE DIVINE KNIFE.
BA (SLICE)
THE BASELARD FROM LILLY.
KNOWL-EDGE FROM EINA-SAN.
GO (STOMP)

AND...
G!!!! (CLANG)
...THE TECHNIQUES AIZ-SAN TAUGHT ME!
ZAN (SLASH)
EVERYTHING, EVERYTHING ALL AT ONCE!
I'LL HIT IT WITH ALL I'VE GOT...

...AND IT WILL...
...FALL!!!

ANY ONE OF THEM COULD HAVE ENDED THE FIGHT IN AN INSTANT.

EVEN SO, THEY COULD NOT.

THEIR INSTINCTS AS ADVENTURERS WOULDN'T ALLOW IT.

THOSE INSTINCTS DEMANDED THEY OBSERVE THIS FIGHT TO ITS CONCLUSION.

THAT BOY'S SPEED AND PHYSICAL STRENGTH ARE BEYOND THAT OF A LEVEL-ONE ADVENTURER.
EVEN SO, THEY DON'T MATCH THAT OF A LEVEL-TWO MINOTAUR.
THERE'S ONLY ONE THING KEEPING THIS FIGHT AS CLOSE AS IT IS—

HIS COURAGE.

A MOMENT'S HESITATION WOULD BE FATAL.
IT'S HIS SHOCKINGLY STRONG RESOLVE ALLOWING HIM TO PUSH TO THE ABSOLUTE LIMIT...
...AND COMMIT HIMSELF ENTIRELY.

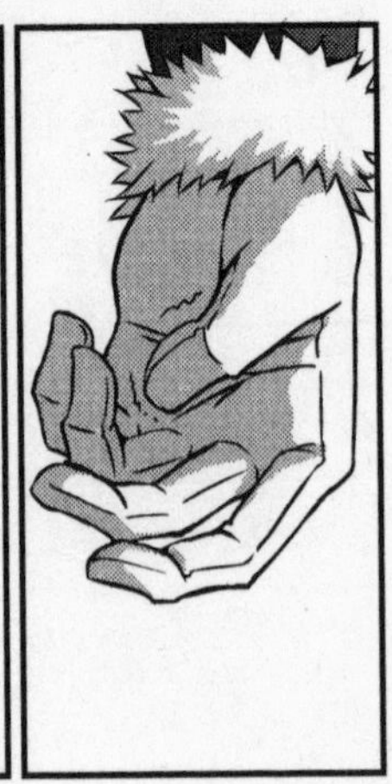

TO THINK THAT I, "BRAVER" FINN DEIMNE, WOULD BE INSPIRED BY ANOTHER ADVENTURER'S COURAGE...
GYUU (CLENCH)

THIS KID IS GOOD.

REALLY GOOD ...!!

CHIRI (TWITCH)
...!!
I GOT SUCKED IN...!?
INTO A FIGHT LIKE THIS? ME...!?

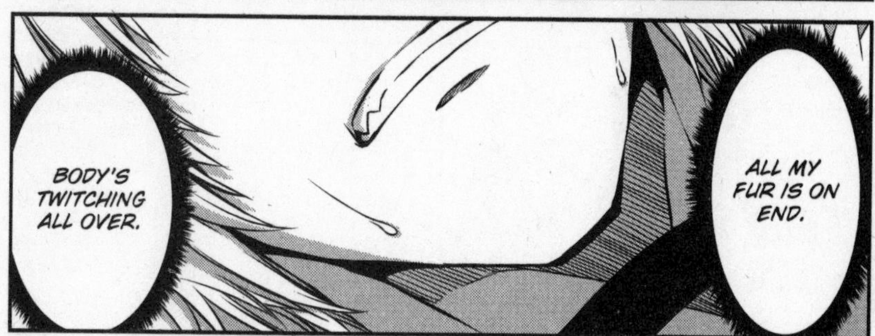
ALL MY FUR IS ON END.
BODY'S TWITCHING ALL OVER.

DAMN IT...

WHAT'S WITH THIS KID...?
WHY'S A WEAKLING LIKE HIM MAKIN' ME...

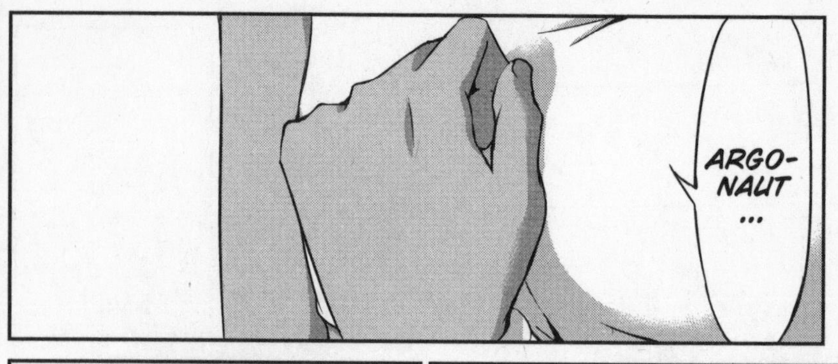
ARGO-
NAUT
...

IT'S A FAIRY TALE ABOUT A YOUNG MAN WHO DREAMED OF BECOMING A HERO AND SLEW A BULL MONSTER TO SAVE A PRINCESS.
HE WAS TRICKED AND USED ALONG THE WAY...
...BUT HIS FRIENDS AND FAIRIES HELPED HIM...
...UNTIL HE FINALLY RESCUED HER.
...HE'S A STRANGE HERO.
BUT I LOVED HIS STORY...

FAIRY TALE...

MOTHER...

DO YOU LIKE THIS STORY?

I DON'T KNOW.
I DON'T UNDERSTAND...

...A SINGLE THING...
...AND YET...

...LOOK
AWAY.

BOBOBOU (BOOM)
FIREBOLT!!
THAT WAS QUICK!
ONE OF THOSE SHORT-TRIGGER SPELLS!?
DID HE EVEN CAST A TRIGGER SPELL!?
HE'S PUTTING UP ONE HECK OF A FIGHT...
... BUT ...
HAAH...
HAAH...
HAAH...
HIS OPPONENT... IS TOO STRONG.

VOO
(ROAR)

THAT MINOTAUR...

...ISN'T NORMAL EITHER...!!

THAT CASTING SPEED IS IMPRESSIVE, HOWEVER...
BELL-SAMA ...!
IT'S NOT ENOUGH ...!
...MINOTAUR HIDE NATURALLY RESISTS BOTH HEAT AND COLD. IT WON'T TAKE DAMAGE.

THAT KNIFE AND MAGIC AREN'T GONNA DO IT.
ARE YOU SAYING HE'S DONE FOR!?
IT'S TOO SOON TO CALL ...
...IS WHAT I'D LIKE TO SAY.

BAKI (SNAP)

HIS WEAPON IS DONE FOR.
!!
BI (FLING)

GIN
(CLANG)

NEED A WEAPON? THERE'S ONE...
...RIGHT HERE!!
DO
(STAB)

VOOO (HOWL)

BUCHI (RIP)
BUCHI
BUCHI
BUCHI
NGHH!!

BIBA (BURST)
GRAHH!!

ZAN (THUD)
VOOOO

FIRE-
BOLT!!
KA
(FLASH)
BOU
(BOOM)
BOBOBO
(BANG)
ZU
(HISS)

AAAAAARGH!!

GAHH!!
DO (SLASH)

HE GOT A HIT!!

NGH GAHH!!
DO
DO
DO
DO
DO

WHOA! HE SUCKS ...!
BUT HE'S PUSH-ING IT BACK.
GO (SLAM)
AAAAAAGHH!!
GA (THUD)
GA
GA
GA
GA
GA
GA
GROOOOAH!!

MY BODY FEELS LIGHT.
MY MIND IS WORKING AT MAX CAPACITY.

MY HEART IS ON FIRE.
FOWARD.
FOWARD.
TCH!
FOWARD.

PUSH FORWARD!!
GO (WHAM)

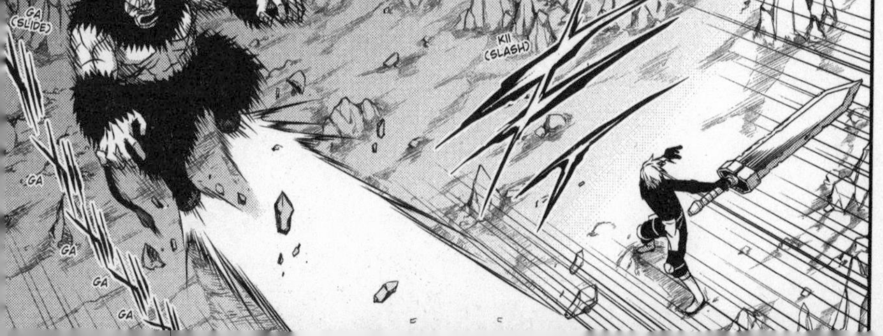
GA (SLIDE)
KII (SLASH)
GA
GA
GA
GA

GA (SLAM)

HIT THE ENEMY IN FRONT OF ME WITH EVERYTHING I HAVE.

I'VE NEVER FELT THIS WAY BEFORE.
THIS DESIRE TO BE A HERO WHO'S STRONG ENOUGH TO DEFEAT THIS THING—

SURPASS MY WEAK SELF.
GO BEYOND THE ME THAT ONLY DREAMS ABOUT THIS.
EXCEED MY LIMITS.

FOWARD!

PRESS AHEAD!!!

HAAAAAHH!
VOOO (ROAR)

BEYOND THE LIMIT...

...BEYOND— THAT LIMIT!

BREAK...

...THROUGH!!!

FIREBOLT!!

BOU
(FWOOM)
HFF...
BO
FIREBOLT!!

IT WAS THE TYPE OF BATTLE ALL ADVENTURERS DREAMED OF.

ONLY THEY HAD FOR-GOT-TEN ...
...OR LOST THE SPARK.

YET IT STILL SMOLDERED DEEP WITHIN THEIR HEARTS—

FI-IREBOOOLT!!

A PURE WHITE, BURNING PASSION.

HE... HE WON.
...MIND DOWN.
H...HE'S UNCON-SCIOUS BUT STILL STAND-ING...

HIS NAME IS BELL CRANELL.
I WAS TOLD YOU RECENTLY RESCUED HIM FROM A MINOTAUR ON FLOOR FIVE.
DAAAAAH!
BI (FLINCH)
FOR ALL THE TIMES YOU SAVED ME...
THANK YOU SO VERY MUCH!!
...I GUESS IT'S BECAUSE I HAVE A GOAL I WANT TO AC-COMPLISH...
...AT ALL COSTS.

BELL CRANELL...
AIZ WOULD NEVER FORGET THAT NAME.

Is it WRONG to TRY to PICK UP GIRLS IN A DUNGEON? ON THE SIDE

Sword Oratoria

DUNGEON FLOOR FIFTY SAFE POINT BASE CAMP
quest 36. Full Speed into the Depths

URO (PACE)
URO
URO
URO

KURUN (FLIP)

WHAT'S GOING ON WITH BETE-SAN AND THE OTHERS ...?
THAT'S WHAT I WANNA KNOW...
EVERY-ONE'S EVEN MORE INTENSE THAN NORMAL ...

BASIC ABILITIES... ARE ALL "S"...!!?
A STATUS THAT BROKE THE LIMIT...
UNBELIEVABLY FAST GROWTH...
IF A SKILL IS MAKING THAT POSSIBLE...
...I WANT TO KNOW.
I...
...WANT TO GET STRONGER... TOO.

DON'T.
!
WHAT HAS BEEN REVEALED CAN'T BE HELPED, BUT...
...TO GO ANY FURTHER WOULD BE IMPROPER.
...
... SORRY.
... FINN.
PLEASE LET ME TAKE THESE TWO BACK TO THE SURFACE.
...I'LL CATCH BACK UP.

WHY'S EVERYONE BEEN SO WEIRD COMING DOWN HERE?

WE SAW THIS REALLY AMAZING ADVENTUR-ER ON OUR WAY TO THE EIGHTEENTH FLOOR.
HAVEN'T BEEN ABLE TO SIT STILL SINCE!

OH?
SOUNDS LIKE A SWORDSMAN I'D LIKE TO SNATCH UP FOR MYSELF.
YOU CATCH THE NAME?

UHH... CRELL BANELL?
?
HO-HO, I'LL MAKE A NOTE OF THAT ONE...
DINNER'S READY —!

LET'S BEGIN OUR FINAL MEETING, SHALL WE?

AS STATED PREVIOUSLY, ONLY A SELECT FEW WILL BE CONTINUING PAST THE FIFTY-FIRST FLOOR.
EVERYONE ELSE, INCLUDING HEPHAISTOS FAMILIA, WILL STAY HERE TO GUARD THE CAMP.
THIS PARTY WILL INCLUDE MYSELF ...
... RIVERIA, GARETH ...

...AIZ, TIONA ...
... TIONE ...
... BETE ...

AS FOR SUPPORTERS— RAUL, NARFI...
... ALICIA, CRUZ...

...AND LEFIYA.

FOR THOSE REMAINING AT CAMP, SHOULD ANY OF THOSE NEW SPECIES OF MONSTERS APPEAR...
...FEND THEM OFF FROM A DISTANCE USING MAGIC SWORDS AND SPELLS.
DO NOT LET THEM GET CLOSE TO CAMP.

AKI, I'M LEAVING YOU IN CHARGE.
YES, SIR!

TSUBAKI WILL BE JOINING THE PARTY TO TEND TO OUR WEAPONS.
LEAVE IT TO ME.
NOW SEEMS LIKE A GOOD TIME TO HAND THESE OUT!

AS RE-QUESTED...
DURAN-DALS.
ALWAYS THOUGHT A DURANDAL'D BE HEAVIER.

WHAT, YOU DIDN'T REQUEST ANOTHER VERSION OF THAT STUPIDLY MASSIVE THING YOU CALL A WEAPON?
DIDN'T HAVE A CHOICE!
GOT TOLD SHE WOULDN'T FINISH EVERYONE'S STUFF IN TIME FOR THE EXPEDITION IF I GOT SOMETHING LIKE URGA.
T-TIONE-SAN...
YOU GOT A HALBERD ...?
WELL, YOU KNOW. FIGURED SOME-THING LIKE THIS WOULD BE BETTER AGAINST THE CRITTERS WE'LL BE UP AGAINST ON THE FIFTY-FIRST FLOOR.
I CALL IT THE ROLAND SERIES. EACH ONE OF THEM COMES EXACTLY AS ORDERED.

I USED ONLY THE BEST MATERIALS!
THERE ARE A FEW DIFFERENCES HERE AND THERE DEPENDING ON THE SHAPE, BUT I GUARANTEE AT LEAST SECOND-TIER ATTACK POWER OUTTA EACH ONE.
THANKS, TSUBAKI.
THIS IS EXACTLY WHAT I WANTED.

WE SHOULD ADJOURN TO PREPARE FOR TO-MORROW.
WE WILL SET OUT AT THE GUARD CHANGE AT 4 A.M.

KENKI. LEMME LOOK AT THAT WEAPON OF YERS.
I'M SURE IT COULD USE A BIT OF SERVICE.

......
...THANK YOU.

SO THAT LITTLE GIRL'S ALL GROWN UP AND REPRE-SENTING THE CITY NOW, HUH?
SHA (SCRAPE)
SHA
SHA
SHOULD'A CALLED DIBBS ON YA, YEAH?
WHAT A WASTE.
SHA
SHA
SHA

...NAH, THAT'S A LIE.
I'M GONNA BE FRANK WITH YA, KENKI.
BACK THEN, I NEVER IMAGINED WANTIN' TO CRAFT A WEAPON FOR YOU.

TEN YEARS AGO... WAIT, WAS IT NINE?
YOU WERE JUST LIKE A NAKED SWORD BACK THEN.
FIGHT-ING AND FIGHTING, NO MATTER HOW MUCH DAMAGE YOUR BLADE TOOK...
I REMEMBER THINKIN'... "THAT GIRL'S GONNA GET HERSELF KILLED."

WHAT'S THE POINT IN MAKING A WEAPON...
...FOR ADVEN-TURERS WHO SWING THEM SINGLE-MINDEDLY?

I......

I'LL TELL YA. THOSE FOLKS DON'T THINK OF YOU AS A WEAPON WIELDER...
...THEY THINK OF YOU AS THE WEAPON ITSELF.

YOU KNOW, I FOUND IT VERY IRONIC WHEN THE GODS GAVE YOU THAT ALIAS, "SWORD PRINCESS."

I WAS WONDERING WHEN YOU'D FINALLY BREAK.

AIZ...
...THOSE WHO PUSH WHILE RUNNIN' FULL TILT WILL ALWAYS TRIP.
SO DON'T GO FORGET-TIN'.
BUT YOU'VE CHANGED.
HUH ...?

YOU'VE MEL-LOWED OUT.
PEOPLE WHO DON'T KNOW YA MIGHT STILL SAY YOU LOOK LIKE A DOLL, BUT YOUR FACE REALLY IS SOFTER.
PASHA (SPLASH)

DO YOU... THINK I'VE BECOME WEAK?
YOU'VE GOTTEN STRONGER, HAVEN'T YA?
JUST LOOK AT YOUR LEVEL, SHOOTING UP LIKE IT HAS.
THAT'S NOT WHAT I MEAN.

SO MAYBE YOU'VE LOST YOUR EDGE.
BUT FOR A SWORD, THAT MEANS YOU FOUND YER SCABBARD.
WHEN IT'S SAFE IN ITS SHEATH, A SWORD DOESN'T NEED TO BE SHARP AS A TACK ALL OF THE TIME.
THEN WHEN YOU'RE FACING AN ENEMY YOU NEED TO KILL...
...YOU CAN FLASH RIGHT OUT AT 'EM.
WHAT IT ALL COMES DOWN TO IS YER FRIENDS.

BI
(SWISH)
BA
(FWIP)
BA
BA
BA
BA
BA
GRRR... IT JUST DOESN'T FEEL RIGHT IF IT ISN'T URGA!
DIDN'T I TELL YA TO GET SOME REST, MISSY?
OH, GARETH.
BUT...
...I'M ALL WOUND UP... CAN'T SIT STILL AT ALL.

'COS OF THAT LAD YA SAW ON YOUR WAY DOWN?

YEAH!
IT WAS JUST SO AMAZING!!
KURU (SPIN)
LIKE A HERO STRAIGHT OUTTA LEGEND!
HE WENT UP AGAINST THAT BIG THING KNOWING HE WAS NO MATCH AND BEAT IT ANYWAY!

TOMORROW I'M GONNA FIGHT JUST LIKE HIM!
...AND I'LL PROTECT AIZ, LEFIYA, EVERYBODY!!

SEEMS I'M WORRYIN' OVER NOTHIN', HUH...?

SHALL WE HAVE A BIT OF A SPAR, THEN?
REALLY!?
AS LONG AS YA HIT THE HAY RIGHT AFTER.

BUSTU (MUMBLE)
BUTSU
BUTSU
BUTSU
BUTSU
BUTSU
I WILL NOT SLOW DOWN AIZ AND THE OTHERS...
...I CANNOT FAIL. I SIMPLY CANNOT FAIL TOMORROW.
A LITTLE TENSE, ARE WE?
BIKU (FLINCH)
EEP!?
PO (PAT)

TIONE-SAN!? WHEN DID YOU COME IN!?
A WHILE AGO. PAY ATTENTION...
GOOD THING THE CAPTAIN ASKED ME TO CHECK IN...
HUH? THE CAPTAIN...?
IT'S NOTHING.
WHAT ARE YOU DOING IN HERE?
I... UHH...
...WAS MEDITATING TO ENSURE I DID NOT FAIL TOMORROW...

!?
GUN (GRAB)
ガッ

LEFIYA.
YE... YESSH!?
REMEMBER WHAT AIZ SAID ON THE FIFTY-FIRST FLOOR?
WE WILL PROTECT YOU...
...SO LIE BACK AND TAKE IT EASY.

AND WHAT IS IT THAT WILL SAVE US...?

...MY... MAGIC...!

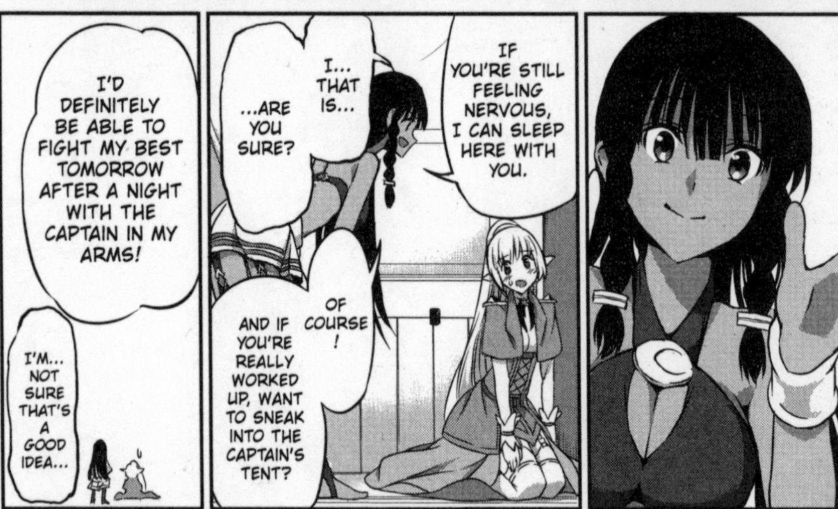
IF YOU'RE STILL FEELING NERVOUS, I CAN SLEEP HERE WITH YOU.
I... THAT IS...
...ARE YOU SURE?
OF COURSE!
AND IF YOU'RE REALLY WORKED UP, WANT TO SNEAK INTO THE CAPTAIN'S TENT?
I'D DEFINITELY BE ABLE TO FIGHT MY BEST TOMORROW AFTER A NIGHT WITH THE CAPTAIN IN MY ARMS!
I'M... NOT SURE THAT'S A GOOD IDEA...

NOT GOOD... THIS IS NOT GOOD!
BUTSU (MUMBLE)
BUTSU
BUTSU
BUTSU
BUTSU
BUTSU
COME ON, RAUL. PULL YOURSELF TOGETHER.
A... AKI...
THIS ISN'T THE FIRST TIME YOU'RE GOING PAST THE FIFTY-FIRST FLOOR, RIGHT?
YOU'VE COME BACK ALIVE EVERY TIME. HAVE A LITTLE FAITH IN YOURSELF!
ANAKITY AUTUMN
NICKNAME: AKI
LEVEL FOUR, SECOND-TIER ADVENTURER. JOINED LOKI FAMILIA AT THE SAME TIME AS RAUL. LEVELHEADED WITH NERVES OF STEEL.
BUT...
...LAST TIME, THAT NEW SPECIES NEARLY KILLED ME, SO WHAT IF THEY FINISH THE JOB...?
AKI... IF I DON'T MAKE IT BACK...
...PLEASE SEND THE MONEY I GOT SAVED UP IN MY ROOM TO MY FAMILY BACK HOME...
NOT THIS AGAIN...

UM...

IS IT REALLY SO DANGEROUS DOWN THERE? PAST FLOOR FIFTY-ONE?

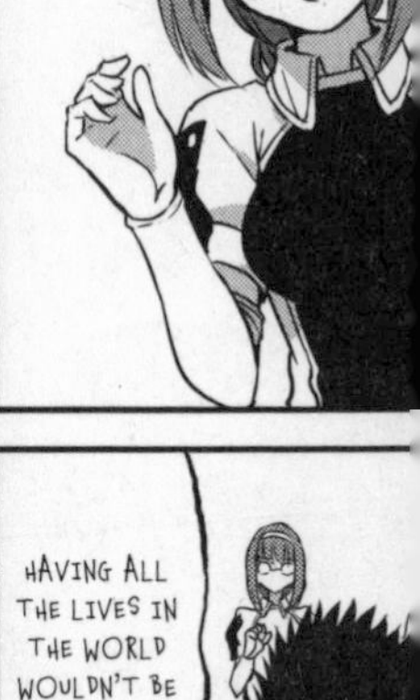

HAVING ALL THE LIVES IN THE WORLD WOULDN'T BE ENOUGH.

DESCENDING INTO THE FIFTY-SECOND FLOOR IS LIKE DROPPING INTO HELL ITSELF.
EVERYTHING YOU THOUGHT YOU KNEW FROM THE PAST FIFTY FLOORS GOES OUT THE DOOR.

RAUL, YOU SHOULDN'T SCARE THEM LIKE THAT.
TO DO SO IS A FAILURE IN YOUR DUTY AS A SUPERIOR.

R-RIVERIA-SAN... I'M SORRY.
YOU ALL HAVE NOTHING TO FEAR.
IN THE EVENT THAT NEW SPECIES DO APPEAR...
...SIMPLY PICK THEM OFF FROM A DIS-TANCE.

OR ARE YOU SAYING YOU WON'T BE ABLE TO HANDLE THAT?

JUST WAIT PATIENTLY FOR OUR RETURN.
CAN I EXPECT SOMETHING BIG, RIVERIA-SAN?
AH, YES. WE'LL BE BRINING SOUVENIRS FROM THE FIFTY-NINTH FLOOR.
I HOPE YOU'RE ALL EXCITED.
IF YOU'RE GOING BIG, BRING ME BACK A GIANT BONE, PLEASE!
NITWIT! HOW'RE THEY SUPPOSED TO CARRY IT BACK?

I SEE... SHE CAME HERE TO PUT US ALL AT EASE...
...SEEING AS WE NEARLY GOT WIPED OUT HERE LAST TIME...

THAT MUST MEAN FINN AND GARETH ARE ALSO...

I'VE STILL GOT A LONG WAY TO GO...

...ALL RIGHT!
HOW ABOUT A LITTLE PRE-RAID CARD GAME!?
EVERYONE, PLACE YOUR BETS!
WITH A LITTLE LUCK, YOU COULD GO HOME WITH THE JACKPOT!!

DON'T GET CAR-RIED AWAY.
HA-HA-HA-HA-HA!
OOF!!

I DON'T NEED NO FRIGGIN' PEP TALK.

...

WHAT ARE YOU LOOKING AT?

CAN'T YOU TELL?
WHERE WE'RE HEADING TOMORROW— THAT NEST OF FILTHY, DISGUSTING MONSTERS.

WHERE IS IT YOU'VE BEEN LOOKING THESE PAST SIX DAYS?

ZA (SHF)
FINN, PUT ME ON THE FRONT LINE TOMORROW.
I DON'T CARE IF THAT NEW SPECIES OR THAT LADY-CREATURE SHOWS UP.
I'LL CRUSH THEM ALL.

ALL RIGHT.

......
......
IT'S NOT THAT YOU GOT WEAKER.
YOU'VE JUST GOT MORE TO PROTECT NOW.
AND YOU DON'T LIKE BEIN' PROTECTED YOURSELF.

DUNGEON FLOOR ??
GAOOOOO (HOOOWL)
GUOOOOO (GROWL)

GARI (CRUNCH)

WHAT ARE YOU DOING?

GAAAA (ROAR)
DOSU (STAB)
EXACTLY WHAT IT LOOKS LIKE I'M DOING.

BUCHI (SNAP)
BUCHI
I'M EAT-ING.

THE SWORD PRINCESS AND HER ALLIES HAVE BEGUN THEIR EXPEDITION.
ZAA (CHISS)
WHY HAVE YOU DONE NOTHING?
SURELY YOU WELL KNOW...
...THIS BODY CONSUMES DREADFUL AMOUNTS OF ENERGY.

...
I WAS GRAVELY INJURED IN THE BATTLE WITH ARIA AND HER FRIENDS.
I NEED TO REST.

DO WHAT YOU WILL.
BUT SHOULD PROBLEMS ARISE...

THEY'RE STRONG.
MARK MY WORDS, THEY'LL MAKE IT TO THE FIFTY-NINTH FLOOR *WHERE IT AWAITS*.

...IN THE WORST CASE...
...ARIA'S CORPSE WILL BE ENOUGH.

YOU INTEND TO DEFY ENYO?
USE ME ALL YOU WANT.
I DON'T CARE.
ZU (SHF)
BUT IN RETURN, I WILL DO AS I PLEASE.
TCH ...!

LET ENYO KNOW AS WELL.
THAT I MAY NEED TO ACT ON MY OWN FROM TIME TO TIME.
WE'RE DONE HERE. LEAVE ME.
VOOO (HOWL)

DUNGEON FLOOR FIFTY, NEXT MORNING

HOW COME I GOTTA BE ON THE FRONT LINE WITH BETE?
SHUT UP, YA STUPID AMAZON.
HA-HA-HA! YOU GUYS SURE ARE A LIVELY BUNCH AT ALL HOURS!
I'M AFRAID IT'S NOT OUR BEST SIDE.

LEFIYA, YOUR BREATHING IS AWFULLY SHALLOW. TRY TO RELAX.
R-RIGHT!
YOU TOO, RAUL! BE READY WHEN THE TIME COMES.
Y-ES!!

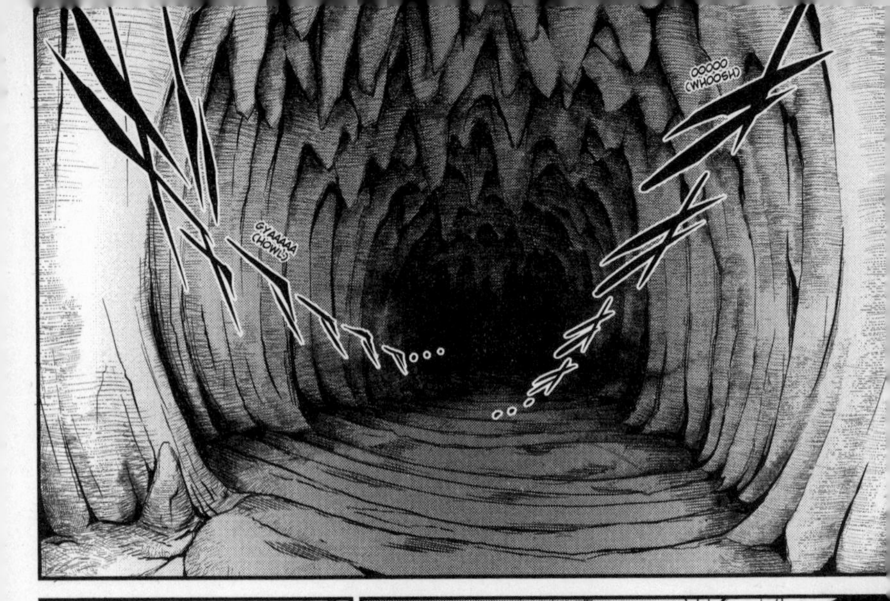
OOOOO (WHOOSH)
GYAAAAA (HOWLS)

THAT'S ENOUGH OF THE IDLE CHATTER.

EVERY-ONE, PREPARE FOR BATTLE.

BETE, TIONA, YOU'RE UP!
DON (FWOOSH)

BORI (CRASH)
GAGA (THUD)

STAY ON THE MAIN ROUTE AS PLANNED!
DON'T LET ANY NEW SPECIES GET CLOSE!!

THEY'RE COMING FROM THE PASSAGE UP AHEAD.
FRONT LINE, KEEP MOVING FOR-WARD!!
AIZ, TIONE! THEY'RE YOURS!
ON IT!!
DON'T GET TOO FAR FROM THE GROUP, YA HEAR!!?

GRAAAAAGH!

THAT WAS MINE, BETE!
B-BETE-SAN IS EVEN WORSE THAN USUAL...

HEH! THE RUMORS DON'T DO HIM JUSTICE.
GAN (SLASH)

TSUBAKI-SAN, HOW DID A SMITH LIKE YOU GET TO BE SO STRONG...?

HMM.

A CRAFTS-MAN'S GOTTA CHECK HER WORK, DON'T SHE?
BAO (SLAM)

GOTTA SEE HOW MANY OF THE DUNGEON'S BEASTIES HER CREATIONS CAN CUT THROUGH.
ZABA (STRIKE)
AT SOME POINT WHEN I WAS FIGURIN' THAT ALL OUT...
OH! SOME-THIN' GOOD!

...I ENDED UP GETTIN' STRONG.
THAT'S MILDLY TERRIFYING.

NARFI, URGA, PLEASE!
YES!
HERE I COME!!
HIIIMAAA!

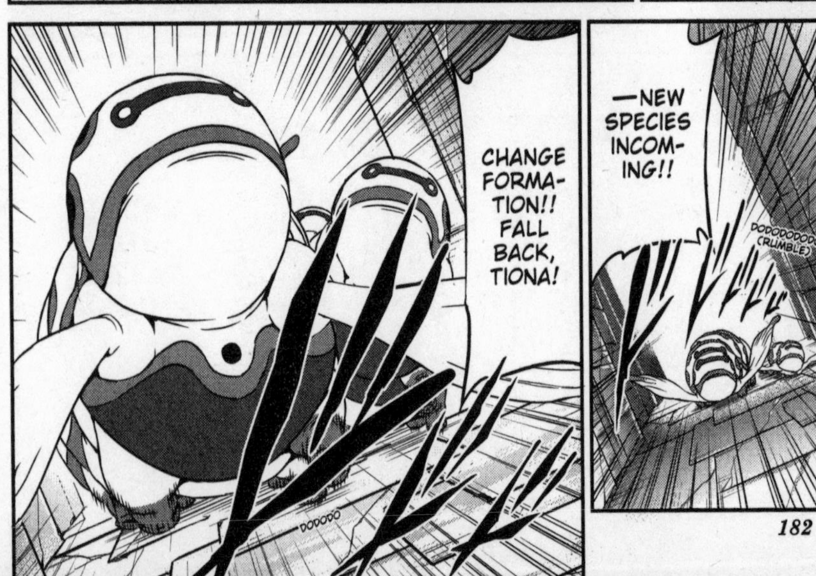
—NEW SPECIES INCOMING!!
DODODODODO (RUMBLE)
CHANGE FORMATION!! FALL BACK, TIONA!
DODODO

AWAKEN, TEMPEST!
AIZ, SEND SOME MY WAY!!
OOOOOOOOHH!
AAA!
OORAAH!

FADING LIGHT, FREEZING LAND.
BLOW WITH THE POWER OF THE THIRD HARSH WINTER.
MY NAME IS ALF!!
EVERYONE, TAKE COVER!

WYNN FIMBULVETR!!
GOA (BOOM)

PAKIKI (CRACKLE)

WHEW! THAT MAGIC WAS A DOOZY!
IF ONLY WE COULD GET THAT KINDA POWER OUTTA A MAGIC SWORD, EH?
THE DAY THAT HAPPENS IS THE DAY I LOSE MY POSITION...

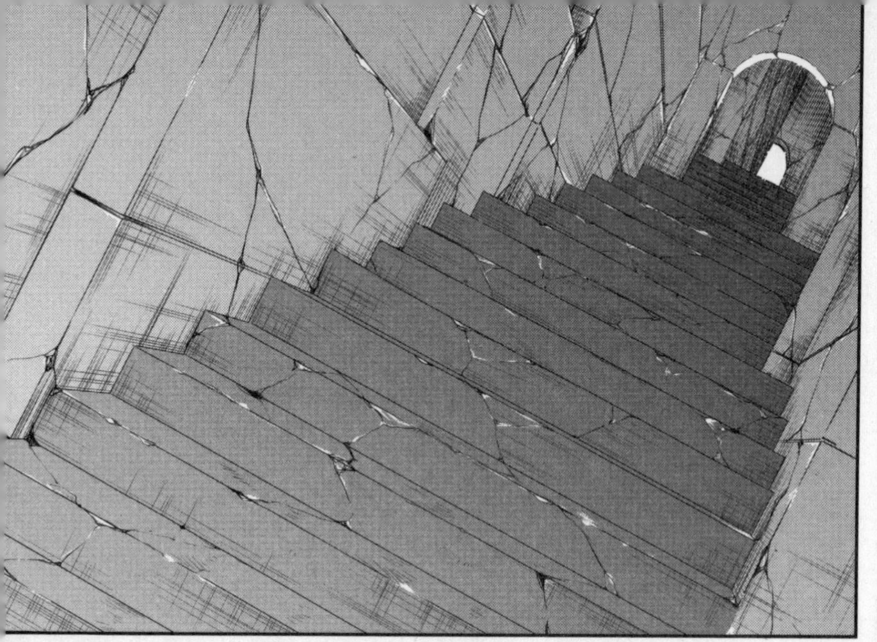

AT LAST, THE ENTRANCE TO THE FIFTY-SECOND FLOOR.

THERE WILL BE NO REPLENISHING FROM HERE ON OUT.
LET'S GO.
DA (JUMP)

AVOID COMBAT WHEREVER POSSIBLE!
SIMPLY REPELLING MONSTERS IS FINE!!
MOST OF ALL, DON'T GET SNIPED!!

PICK UP THE PACE!!
I AIN'T NEVER BEEN THIS FAR DOWN.
IS IT TRUE?
THE *SNIPING*?

GUROOOO (HOWL)

FINN!
YES —
WE'VE BEEN SPOTTED.
MOVE! MOVE!!
...A DRAGON'S HOWL?
BUT FROM WHERE ...?
...BE- LOW?

IT'S COM- ING.
BETE! CHANGE COURSE!!

ZU
(BAM)

DO
DO
DO
DO (RUMBLE)
DO
MAKE A DETOUR!! TO THE WESTERN ROUTE!!

I DON'T CARE IF WE DRAW IN THOSE CATERPIL-LARS!!
RIVERIA, WE NEED A PRO-TECTION SPELL!!
TREE SPIRITS— HEAR MY PRAYER. GOWN OF THE FOREST!
HOW MANY !?
SIX... NO, SEVEN AT LEAST!!

IT'S... IT'S TRUE!
I'VE HEARD ALL ABOUT IT, BUT ...!
THE REALITY IS SO MUCH WORSE !!
RAUL, WATCH OUT!!

RAUL-SAN !!
DO (SLAM)

GUN (VOOM)

GYUKI (YOINK)
LEFIYA!?
GA (GAPE)

ZU (BLAST)

ATTACKED FROM BELOW.
IN THE PAST, WHEN ZEUS FAMILIA REIGNED IN ORARIO...
...THEY SET THE RECORD FOR THE DEEPEST DUNGEON FLOOR REACHED AND NICKNAMED THIS AREA...
..."THE DRAG-ON'S URN."

VALGANG DRAGON—
FROM THE DRAGONS ON THE FIFTY-EIGHTH FLOOR, AT THE VERY BOTTOM OF THE URN...
...COMES AN ATTACK AIMED HUN-DRED OF MEDERS AWAY TO THE FIFTY-SECOND FLOOR...

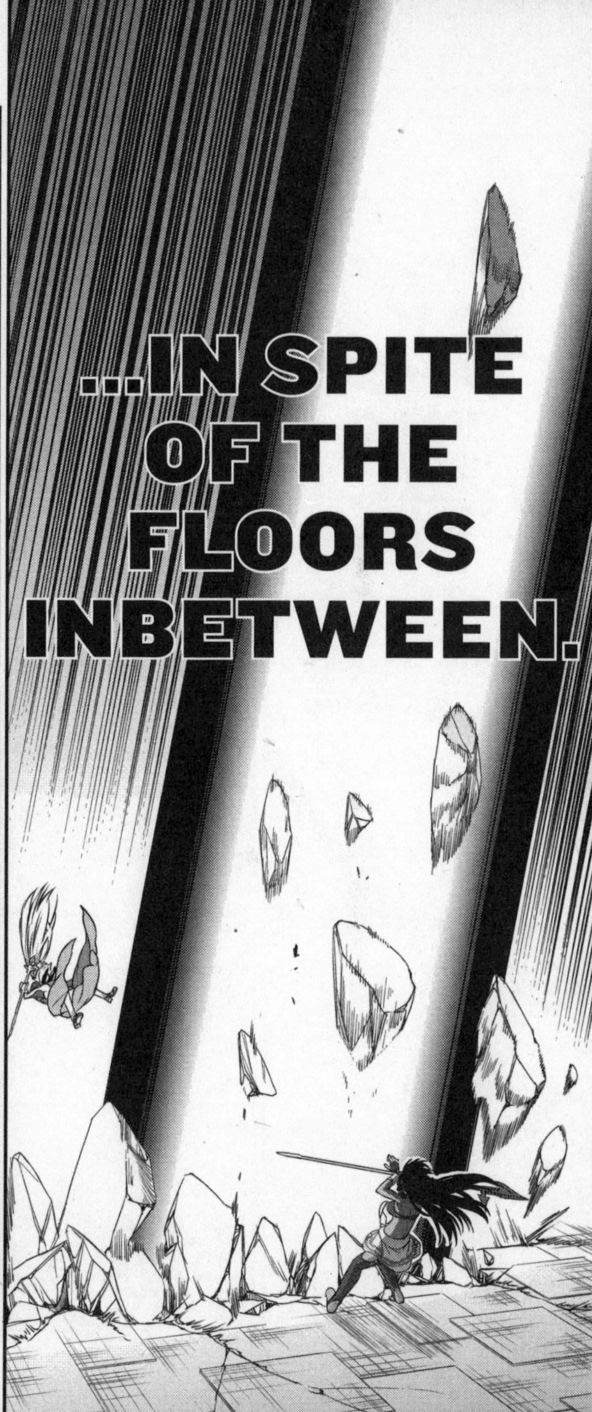
...IN SPITE OF THE FLOORS INBETWEEN.

I CAN'T ...
... SLOW DOWN.

I'M FALLING.

EVERYTHING YOU THOUGHT YOU KNEW FROM THE PAST FIFTY FLOORS GOES OUT THE DOOR.

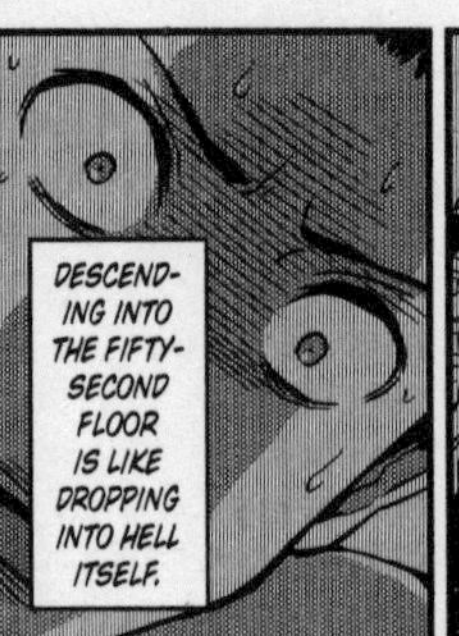
DESCENDING INTO THE FIFTY-SECOND FLOOR IS LIKE DROPPING INTO HELL ITSELF.

THE SCALE IS DIFFERENT.
THE WHOLE MAGNITUDE IS WRONG.
PERIL ON A COMPLETELY DIFFERENT LEVEL.

IS THIS THE DUNGEON!!?

IS THIS THE REAL...

...HELL!!!?
Sword Oratoria 9 End

PARTY CHOSEN TO ADVANCE BELOW FLOOR FIFTY-ONE

AIZ WALLENSTEIN

"SWORD PRINCESS"
Lv. 6

LEFIYA VIRIDIS

"THOUSAND ELF"
Lv. 3

TSUBAKI COLLBRANDE

CAPTAIN OF HEPHAISTOS FAMILIA
"CYCLOPS"
Lv. 5

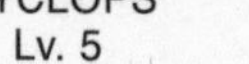

RAUL NORD
"HIGH NOVICE"
Lv. 4

ALICIA FORESTLIGHT
Lv. 4

CRUZ BUSSELL
Lv. 4

NARFI ROHR
Lv. 4

THANK YOU FOR PURCHASING *SWORD ORATORIA* VOLUME 9!
THE BATTLE FROM FLOOR FIFTY-TWO WILL CONTINUE IN THE NEXT VOLUME.
DID THE NOVEL'S INTENSITY COME ACROSS!? DRAWING THE NEXT VOLUME WILL
SURELY BE A BATTLE LIKE I'VE NEVER KNOWN BEFORE!!
PLEASE COME BACK AND SEE FOR YOURSELF!!

TAKASHI YAGI

Coming up...
BASHU (SLASH)
DO (THUD)
AIZ, DON'T GO!
LOKI FAMILIA SEPARATED, AND AIZ IS OFF AHEAD.
LEFIYA PLUMMETS.
DIE.
YOU KIDDOS STILL WITH US?
GARETH!?
OLD MAN!?

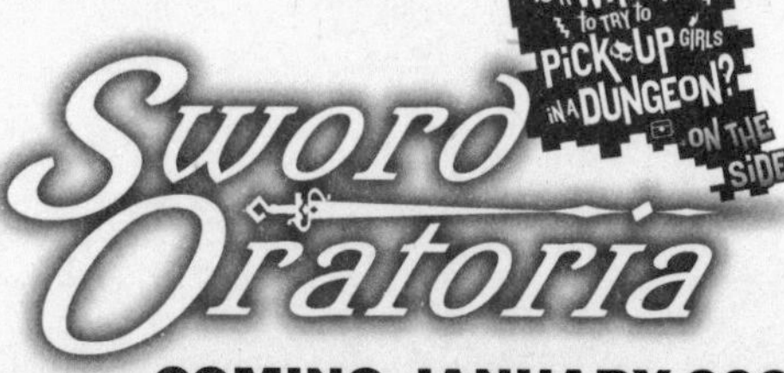

COMING JANUARY 2020!

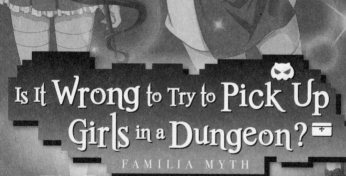

FINAL FANTASY®
ファイナルファンタジー ロスト・ストレンジャー
LOST STRANGER
Keep up with the latest chapters in the simul-pub version! Available now worldwide wherever e-books are sold!

Yen Press